Haiku Ponderings

A Haiku Collection for Pondering Life

By Anthony Nanfito

While every precaution has been taken in the preparation of this book, the publisher assumes no responsibility for errors or omissions, or for damages resulting from the use of the information contained herein.

HAIKU PONDERINGS

First edition. June 7, 2021.

Written by Anthony Nanfito.

To all of the health care workers around the globe.

Introduction

During the year of 2020, writing haiku each day helped me stay grounded in a world that seemed to be falling apart. It gave me a moment to be present and think about what I value, what is important to me, and how to give back to others. It is amazing what can be revealed to you in seventeen syllables. As much as I wanted the world to calm down and go back to the calmness that came before, haiku gave me an anchor to hold onto and ride out the waves.

In the universe we inhabit, the laws of physics forbid me from changing my temporal position—other than permanently forward—in the space-time continuum (as much as it would be interesting to do so). It leaves me trapped here in the present moment, yet I do not always exist *here*. Often, I find myself thinking about the future and what is to come. It is one of the many reasons I love reading and writing future-based science fiction. Yet, I have often caught myself dwelling and reliving events of the past too—both joyful and melancholy moments. But the truth is, I—like all other creatures on this planet—am a being of the present moment. Trapped in the here and now by the laws of the universe. Slowly moving forward toward the unknowable future.

However, being trapped in the present is not such a terrible thing. Through writing haiku, I have learned what counts most of all *is* the present moment. The moment of here and now. Since we are forever trapped here—and we never get a redo—we must appreciate the current moment and give more attention to it. That is, we must make the most of it.

In writing the haiku for this book, I have attempted to capture the energy of these priceless moments that are experienced only once, but get to be relived again and again in memoriam. I hope they inspire you to appreciate each and every moment you experience and to be more present with everything that exists around you.

Enclosed within the book, you will find over one hundred haiku and five mini essays—or ponderings—focused on the topics of Mindfulness, Compassion, Gratitude, Love & Loss, and Give & Forgive. At the end of each chapter I have left questions for you to ponder. There is no obligation for you to answer them, unless you want to. Their purpose is to offer you a moment of self-reflection as you think about your own life and how to live it with more mindfulness, compassion, and gratitude. In that spirit, here is the first haiku:

Stuck in the present

Forward moving forever

We live in the now

Chapter 1: Mindfulness

The tree standing tall

Ever reaching to the sky

But always rooted

No matter the season, no matter the weather a tree always reaches for the light. That is its purpose.

As humans, I think there is tremendous value in studying nature because it can teach us how to best live our own lives—especially during challenging times.

A tree always strives to grow upward but remains rooted and grounded. Even during the times of year when it loses it leaves. Barren—it still remains firm to its purpose and waits for the day when the weather warms and the sun shines again.

This is the lesson I have taken from trees. This is the lesson that inspired this haiku.

1

The sky is bright blue

Birds chirp and chatter around

A fine day it is

2

The crunch of the leaves

The soft whistle of the wind

A walk in the woods

3

I hear the birds sing

I feel the sun on my skin

The world is alive

4

Tall purple flowers

Singing birds and buzzing bugs

A lively meadow

5

The army ant climbs

The butterfly flaps its wings

A yard full of life

6

Walking in the field

A dragonfly hovers near

And the grass whispers

7

The birds chirp loudly

The car engines roar and hum

Let the morning start

8

Early morning walk

The sun has not yet risen

The silence still reigns

9

Pigeons peck the ground

An airplane flies overhead

Afternoon outside

10

Basketballs dribble

Children laugh and birds cry out

A day at the park

11

Roaring cars roll by

Hissing buses at bus stops

A city's heartbeat

12

Let go and laugh

Life is short, embrace humor

You always have now

13

A duck walks the shore

The wind rustles the tree leaves

I rest at the pond

14

The tree standing tall

Ever reaching to the sky

But always rooted

15

A lazy Sunday

A slow drizzling rain falls

I sync with nature

16

Cooing cooing birds

Whispering leaves and grasses

Speak less, listen more

17

Squirrels climb tall trees

Children play and birds sing songs

Life is short and long

18

Fallen leaves decaying

Long life lived; branching, rooting

What will I leave behind?

19

The moment we're born

We start to die and decay

Let this guide the day

20

Monks walking the streets

Cars and scooters rolling by

A city wakes up

Questions to Ponder

FOR YOUR OWN REFLECTION or inspiration, ponder the following:

- *How can you remain rooted even when your leaves have fallen?*

- *What are the small moments in your daily life you appreciate? How can you honor them?*

Chapter 2: Compassion

Back to old habits

Falling down stings like acid

Can I get back up?

A lot of my haiku I have written over the past year focus on compassion. Particularly, compassion for others. Even for the smallest of creatures that inhabit our planet. I have written about ants, caterpillars, crickets, spiders, and cockroaches.

We all have opinions about these creatures—some positive, some negative—but regardless of our opinions, these creatures all have a role to play. They all have a purpose.

I have also worked toward extending that compassion to my fellow human beings, including some of the most heinous among us. Extending it towards humans has been more difficult because as creatures with reasoning and intelligence I feel we should know the difference between right and wrong. Yet, even with this we are still fallible and imperfect. And there is one person on this planet that I have continually struggled to extend compassion toward: me.

This haiku speaks to that struggle. At the time I wrote it, I had fallen back to some old, unhealthy habits and I remember mentally berating myself for falling down. Because, as a being who possesses reasoning and intelligence, I felt I should know better.

It has taken some time—a few more haiku and some journaling—but I am starting to accept that, like all the other humans on this planet, I too am fallible. I make mistakes. I fall down. And that is okay. Being fallible does not make me less perfect, but more human.

During this process of extending compassion to myself, I have learned that we cannot really extend it to others until we learn to have compassion for ourselves. That is, when we learn to be compassionate toward our self—both with our fortunes and our flaws—it becomes easier to extend it toward other living beings. Even the smallest among us like ants, caterpillars, crickets, spiders, and cockroaches.

This is the lesson I have taken from falling down. This is the lesson that inspired this haiku.

21

I step out the door

The snail is on its commute

Paths cross but no crunch

22

Little red ant

Where do you crawl when it rains?

You can share my home

23

Ant, caterpillar

Two very small tiny things

Brave in a big world

24

Flat empty grass field

Pigeons and crows peck the ground

Together we play

25

Another cockroach

I grab the bowl and paper

Until we meet again

26

A spotted dove's gaze

We size each other up

No threat here, just trust

27

Spiders in corners

Their webs collecting insects

Two helpful roommates

28

The morning traffic

Crawling its way down the road

Will people be late?

29

Cool morning commute

The father drives, the boy sleeps

Yeah, I'm tired too, kid

30

Cool riverside date

Outdoor fashion show music

Crickets can't compete

31

On the busy days

With little time to relax

Remember to breathe

32

The leaves have fallen

But the tree remains rooted

We can do the same

33

Life works in cycles

Endings create beginnings

Learn to move with them

34

We are all human

The good, the bad, the ugly too

We all feel something

35

Ease others' suffering

Learn more than yesterday

Life philosophy

36

I wish I had tried

What I could have built today...

Build for tomorrow

37

Back to old habits

Falling down stings like acid

Can I get back up?

38

Different beliefs

But common humanity

United we stand

39

Toothpick cleaning teeth

A bug crawling on the toothpick

I'm done. It's yours now.

40

Hashtags divide us

Yet we all suffer from pain

Let's open our hearts

Questions to Ponder

FOR YOUR OWN REFLECTION or inspiration, ponder the following:

- *How do you express compassion toward yourself?*

- *How do you express compassion toward others?*

- *What is a small act of compassion you can express today?*

Chapter 3: Gratitude

———

Tendrils wrap the Earth

Video calls to the family

Global connections

We all spent a lot more time on Zoom, or other video chatting services, in 2020 than we probably expected. Many of us also developed zoom fatigue and eye strain.

Yet these tendrils of the internet that wrap around the globe connect us all. Especially to those we love. As someone who lives in a different country than one of my birth, I am especially grateful for those internet tendrils and video chatting technology.

I know connecting through video is not the same as meeting in person, but wow did it save me. I felt isolated a lot during 2020, but my lifelines were the weekly video chats with my cousins, the weekly game nights with my friends, and calls back to the family in the U.S.

I had been living in Thailand since 2018 and I was used to using video calls to chat with friends and family back in the U.S., but that changed in 2020. It became my sole source of communication for almost everything. Especially in the early days of the pandemic.

While reading about the flu pandemic of 1918, I learned about the similar mask-wearing precautions, and lockdowns people had to go through. I am in awe that they did it all without the technology we have today. But I suppose that is a sign of how integrated such technology has become in our lives. For better or for worse.

However, this lack of technology—or more specifically lack of entertainment (yeah! I'm talking about you Netflix)—also explains why cities threw huge parades and celebrated with tossing masks into the air at the end of the 1918 lockdowns. I can imagine those alive in 1918, probably experienced a lot of boredom, anxiety, and stress being cooped up inside with little to do. In much the same way, we had similar experiences.

This comparison and recognition of how times have changed since 1918, has reinforced my gratitude toward the Internet and video calling technology. It has helped me stay connected to those I love while living abroad, but it has also helped me survive a global pandemic unseen by anyone alive today.

This is the lesson I have taken from those tendrils that wrap around the Earth and create the Internet. This is the lesson that inspired this haiku.

41

Ants in my garbage

The Earth's global clean up force

Service loaned to me

42

Footprints in the sand

I think I've been here before

Old path new ideas

43

The air fills my lungs

The coffee fills my stomach

Tiny miracles

44

Lost my job today

But the sun is still shining

New things are waiting

45

Spring cleaning today

Floors but not the corners

Spiders catching bugs

46

The meal on my plate

A lot of hands helped create

Body, soul—nourished

47

The trees respirate

Breathing in bad and out good

Earth's lungs, human's breath

48

Body aches and pains

Body pleasures and protects

Thanks to it, I'm here

49

Touch, sight, hearing, taste

Container of consciousness

The body provides

50

Since my first entrance

You've protected and carried me

Thanks for your service

51

When the world seems dark

Try to find the light in it

Light follows the dark

52

Aircon, grocery stores,

Motor vehicles, and phones

Past kings are jealous

53

Water fills the glass

Life's essential elixir

Hydration fuels me

54

Cold brisk winter air

A big burly overcoat

My faithful partner

55

Ideas fill my mind

My head spins in the chaos

Journal brings order

56

First morning light

Solar rays wash over plants

Life's energy

57

Tendrils wrap the Earth

Video calls to the family

Global connections

58

Final notebook page

Many scribbles and sketches

Long term companion

59

Small pink puffy clouds

A steadily rising sun

The orb that gives life

60

Waking up today

The sun rises, the world breathes

Miracles abound

Questions to Ponder

FOR YOUR OWN REFLECTION or inspiration, ponder the following:

- *What is something big you are grateful for? What is something small you are grateful for? How can you express your gratitude?*

- *Who is someone you are grateful for? How can you express your gratitude to them?*

Chapter 4: Love & Loss

Pain of love cuts deep

You're here today but someday—

You will be absent

In order to truly love someone, you have to face the fear of losing them. Because in this life we live, all people and all things are transient. The people we love. The things we obtain. And the power we accumulate. Nothing lasts forever and all these are temporary. We do not own them, but borrow them. Only to return them when the universe dictates.

Hence, we must accept that the loved ones we hold dear and the things we cherish will someday be gone. This highlights the importance of cherishing the present moment because *it* is the only true possession we have as we live our transient lives.

While it might seem like this leaves us powerless and without possession, I think it does the opposite. Being present and willing to let go of the people and things we cherish—when the time comes—is empowering. It frees us from the stress and anxiety that comes with worrying about losing someone or something.

Once we accept they will be gone, that pain becomes easier to bear. And if, instead, we focus on honoring the present moment with them, we will have all we truly need.

This is the lesson I have taken from loving and losing. This is the lesson that inspired this haiku.

61

Baby jumping spider

Curiously exploring—

Laptop closed. Short life.

62

Trees reach for the sky

While the leaves fall to the ground

Cycles dictate life

63

Birth, growth, decay, death—

All beings are born and die.

The circle of life.

64

A tractor drives in grass

Flat naked land is revealed

Benefits have costs

65

Friends' love calls—

Between them electrons flow

Zoom meeting

66

Without you—

This bed

Is just a bed

67

A growing ember,

Full of potential you are.

Ember extinguished.

68

Stars shine above me

And crickets sing around me

My love's close to me

69

A tree covered park

Fallen leaves blanket the ground

Loss covers a heart

70

Full flower vases

Empty dining room table

The guests have gone home

71

A couple walks outside

A child grows into adulthood

Moments come and go

72

Butterflies flutter

My heart floats and sputters

Coffee date with you

73

Bricks stack up the wall

Walls build up the house and home

Home makes us feel loved

74

Rolling mountain tops

Drifting cloud banks pass us by

With you time slows down

75

Cuddling in bed

Hands wrapped around each other

A lover's embrace

76

Plastic shields divide

Respirators pump and press

A silent goodbye

77

My heart longs for you

What I would give for one day

Faded memories

78

Pain of love cuts deep

You're here today but someday—

You will be absent

79

Message from a friend

Connected across the globe

Worthwhile investment

80

End of an era

My purpose is obsolete

What do I do now?

Questions to Ponder

FOR YOUR OWN REFLECTION or inspiration, ponder the following:

● *When was the last time you said "I love you" to someone you care about?*

● *When was the last time you said "I love you" to yourself?*

● *When was the last time you honored someone no longer present in your life?*

● *Where are the small moments during your day in which you can express love to those you care about and honor the present moment with them?*

Chapter 5: Give & Forgive

———

A bike was stolen

The victim plans their revenge

Free bike repair shop

I was inspired to write this haiku after reading a news story about a man who had his bike stolen and chose to open a free bike repair shop in response to the tragedy that had stricken him.

There are lots of stories like this out in the world. They remind me of the quote which is often attributed to Frank Sinatra, "the best revenge is massive success." However, it should be noted his daughter Nancy Sinatra, in October of 2012, stated in a tweet his quote was actually, "Living well is the best revenge."[1] Regardless, both quotes speak to the idea of how best to seek revenge.

This haiku, the news story about the bike shop, and Frank Sinatra's quote(s) all speak to this idea that we cannot control everything that happens in this world. In fact, most of the events that occur in this world are far beyond our control. But there is one thing we do have control over: our reaction to these events.

The story of a man who was robbed only to create a free bike repair shop and give to others is not only inspiring for his generosity, but also demonstrates how healing it can be when we give to others and forgive those who harmed us. In an alternative timeline, the man who had his bike stolen could have spent the rest of his life suffering in hate and anger—or followed an endless quest for revenge—because of an event which he had no control over. Instead, he chose to make something good out of a tragedy.

This is the lesson I have taken from the importance of giving and forgiving. This is the lesson that inspired this haiku.

81

Lady Bug crawling

Unexpected visitor

Would you like some food?

82

There are good people

There are heinous people too

All spring forth from wombs

83

Levels of privilege

Inequality filled world

Let's lift others up

84

Pocket coins jingle

Beggar with an empty can

I smile with light steps

85

Mistakes in the past

Problems in the present

Let's forgive and grow

86

Raised by our parents

Expectations met and failed

They did their best

87

Gave the wrong advice

Now my friend is hurting lots

Think before I speak

88

Double amputee

A limping beggar stumbles

A gift of crutches

89

Weekend at the bridge

A stranger steps to the edge

A hug stops the fall

90

Plants breathe CO2

Humans exhale CO2

Symbiosis wins

91

An extra bread roll

A stray dog's empty stomach

Tonight hunger's gone

94

A bike was stolen

The victim plans their revenge

Free bike repair shop

93

Mother earth gives all

Land, sea, air—create our home

Let's give back to her

94

Many things to do

Friend's phone call. Do I have time?

Impromptu coffee

95

Yes, mistakes were made.

I have admitted my wrongs.

Are you ready now?

96

Jackets taped to poles

This night is frightfully cold

Homeless man feels warmth

97

A broken down car

A neighbor offers a ride

It takes a village

98

A secret affair

Lost connection, no repair

Stronger from the strife

99

Two cups of tea poured

Warden and prisoner of old

Humanity shared

100

Struggling student

A teacher stays after school

Shoulders of giants

Questions to Ponder

FOR YOUR OWN REFLECTION or inspiration, ponder the following:

- *How can you turn your own suffering into something that benefits you or others?*

- *How often do you forgive those who hurt you?*

- *How often do you forgive yourself?*

Conclusion

———

Thank you for reading my first book of haiku and pondering the questions in each chapter. I hope they have brought a moment of joy to your life, helped you enjoy the present moment, and express more gratitude. I write haiku every day to capture moments that will never come again. They help me be more present, mindful, and grateful. I hope they do the same for you.

If you want to read more of my haiku, I encourage you to follow me on Instagram *@haikubyfifi*[1]. I also host a podcast, *The Haiku Pond*, where I read haiku written by myself and others. Subscribe wherever you listen to podcasts. Learn more at http://anchor.fm/thehaikupond/.

Lastly, I would love to hear your thoughts about the haiku in this book, the podcast, or anything else you want to share. Send an email to:

nanfitospace@gmail.com

Thank you again for taking the time to be present with me. I hope we get another opportunity in the future. Until then, here is one final haiku:

This part has ended.

But with each ending there is—

A new beginning

---

1. *http://instagram.com/haikubyfifi/*

Let's Stay Connected

Monthly Newsletter

I am a creative soul who expresses himself through science fiction stories, haiku, and podcasts. I post this content to my various online platforms, but that can be time-consuming for followers and supporters to keep track of.

To simplify the process, each month I send out a newsletter with a summary of what's happening in *Nanfito Space*.

As a subscriber of the *Nanfito Space* newsletter, you'll get the latest links to my Buy Me A Coffee posts, podcast episodes of Story Time with Fifi, Blinded by Science, and The Haiku Pond, and—of course—news about my upcoming book releases.

Join today and I'll send you a FREE gift.

As an expression of my gratitude for joining my newsletter, I'll send you the short story *2051: Initiative*[1]. This story is a prequel to my debut novel *2149: Emergence*[2] and follows Elizabeth and Alfred Maverik's journey of creating VR.

---

1. *https://anthonynanfito.com/2020/11/21/2051-initiative/*

2. *http://anthonynanfito.com/books/*

Follow the link to sign up and get your free story today: http://mailchi.mp/ ec95629e22a1/nanfitospace.

Author Website

MY AUTHOR WEBSITE IS the central location on the web where you can find additional updates about my books, short stories, podcasts, and more.

Visit http://anthonynanfito.com to see the latest news.

Social

FOR MORE FREQUENT UPDATES follow me on Social Media:

- Instagram: http://www.instagram.com/haikubyfifi

- Twitter: http://www.twitter.com/wordsbyfifi

- Facebook: https://www.facebook.com/wordsbyfifi

- YouTube: http://www.youtube.com/channel/UCSsETsNWOm-HWZAEpIyspxqg

Wander Away from Haiku and Enter the VR

2149: Emergence

Laura Maverik is an orphaned programmer who lives in a virtual reality completely cutoff from the suffering that plagues the world. But how will she cope when a glitch takes her out of her virtual sanctuary and into the real world?

Coming soon to other retailers!

More info at http://anthonynanfito.com/books

---

[1] @NancySinatra. "His quote was "Living well is the best revenge." It was a needlepoint pillow. I think RFK said it originally, not sure @bobbicisse @fondalo" *Twitter*, 11 Oct, 2012 11:34 p.m., twitter.com/NancySinatra/status/256432559267909632?s=20.

Don't miss out!

Visit the website below and you can sign up to receive emails whenever Anthony Nanfito publishes a new book. There's no charge and no obligation.

https://books2read.com/r/B-A-ZNAO-VKHNB

BOOKS 2 READ

Connecting independent readers to independent writers.

About the Author

Anthony Nanfito was born and raised in Northern California. After completing a degree in mathematics, he taught high school mathematics for five years. Now, he lives in Southeast Asia where teaches English as a Second Language and writes books.

His debut novel, "2149: Emergence," was first published in April 2020 and explores the ubiquitous use of virtual reality to save an environmentally damaged planet.

When he's not writing, you can find him reading a book, listening to a science podcast, enjoying a nature walk in a rainforest, or debating whether he should channel his inner-Picard or inner-Janeway by ordering "Tea Earl Grey Hot" or "Coffee Black" at a cafe.

Visit his website http://anthonynanfito.com/ for more info on his latest releases and how to sign-up for his newsletter. Happy reading!

Read more at anthonynanfito.com.